Original title:
Tropical Sunsets and Starlit Nights

Copyright © 2025 Creative Arts Management OÜ
All rights reserved.

Author: Milo Harrington
ISBN HARDBACK: 978-1-80581-561-7
ISBN PAPERBACK: 978-1-80581-088-9
ISBN EBOOK: 978-1-80581-561-7

A Symphony of Color and Light

A parrot yells, 'I'm feeling bright!'
A sunset paints the world with delight.
The ocean waves dance in their show,
While crabs moonwalk, stealing the glow.

Lemons in hats on the beach, they sway,
A dancing pineapple joined the fray.
Coconuts giggle as they drop down,
As seagulls squawk jokes, wearing a frown.

Dance of Fireflies in the Deep Blue

Fireflies waltz in the night so sly,
They blink and twirl, oh my, oh my!
A frog leaps up, joins with a croak,
'In the air, I'm a feather-light bloke!'

Stars chuckle as they peek through the haze,
While crickets serenade laughter and plays.
The moon wears shades, thinking it's so cool,
While the breeze joins in, a jovial fool.

The Night's Whisper on Warm Breeze

A whisper floats on the warm night's breath,
As palms sway gently, stealing the theft.
'You're too tall!' one whispering vine did tease,
While the night giggles, spreading its ease.

Hyacinths prance in their frilly gowns,
Winking at the moon, wearing its crowns.
The warmth makes everyone feel alive,
Till the lazy sloth shows up to jive.

Glimmers of Twilight on Silent Waters

Twilight arrives with a splash and a laugh,
Bubbles of joy in the water's path.
A fish with a mustache swims by so grand,
Tickling the lily pads, they all stand.

Reflections shimmer as turtles give cheer,
While frogs compose symphonies so near.
The night splashes colors like a painter's brush,
While the wind joins in for a giggling hush.

Twilight's Embrace

The sun dips low, what a sight,
Beach chairs wobble in delight.
Sandy feet take on the glow,
A seagull steals my nacho show.

Palm trees sway, doing the dance,
While crabs plot an escape chance.
A coconut drops on my head,
"Guess I won't use that spot for bed!"

Celestial Dusk

Stars peek out, 'Hey, what's up?'
Fish jump high, they drink from cups.
The moon's got jokes up its bright sleeve,
And clouds all giggle, hard to believe.

A firefly flirts, 'Wink at me!'
I miss it; my aim's a bit fuzzy.
The night is young, with laughs galore,
But I'm quite sure, I flopped before.

Shadows of Paradise

A hammock swings with style so fine,
As I sip on a fruity brine.
Lizards laugh and join the game,
While I forget my own name!

With every sip, I grin and sway,
A beach ball bounces in dismay.
The shadows stretch, they start to tease,
"Hey, lighten up! Get off your knees!"

Radiant Horizons

The horizon glows, a funny hue,
My drink spills out, oh, what to do?
A dolphin rolls by like a pro,
'Guess I'll just keep the show on low!'

As laughter echoes, waves come near,
The gulls squawk loudly, "What's for dinner?"
I've gone from sipping to wide-eyed fun,
Life's a blast under the setting sun!

Serenade of Colors

The sky is a painter, oh what a sight,
With splashes of orange, it just feels right.
A bird in a sombrero, sipping on punch,
Laughs at the clouds, ready for lunch.

The sun takes a bow, it's time to retreat,
While crabs in a conga line dance on the heat.
A laughter erupts from the beachy brigade,
As flip-flops take flight in a wild escapade.

Under a Canopy of Stars

Stars twinkle like diamonds, bursting to chat,
They giggle and wiggle, a cosmic format.
The moon wears pajamas, so fluffy and bright,
While comets do cartwheels, oh what a night!

A fish with a bowtie starts cooking a tune,
Calls over the crickets, they waltz 'neath the moon.
The cicadas are DJs, dropping a beat,
While candles on beaches have found their own feet.

Mellow Hues

The sky blushes softly, like a shy little mate,
Its colors like jellybeans share a sweet fate.
Palms wave like dancers in a rhythmic fun,
While piña coladas invite everyone.

Clouds wear top hats, fancied and cool,
As a squirrel serves drinks, breaking the rule.
The breeze whispers jokes, oh what a delight,
And seashells tell tales of a sparkly night.

The Last Light

The sun does a shimmy, says, 'Time to go!',
While shadows are stretching, putting on a show.
The sand tickles toes, with a silly goodbye,
As fireflies blink like they've had too much pie.

The parrots all giggle, locked in a chase,
They argue on colors, it's a bright freestyle race.
As night drapes its blanket, all snug and tight,
Let's toast with our snacks, what a hilarious night!

Elysian Mornings

The sky wears orange, quite a sight,
Birds complain, "Why's the alarm so bright?"
Coffee spills as I hop and dance,
A sun-soaked wiggle, oh what a chance!

Palm trees laugh, they join the show,
While flip-flops chase a cockatoo's glow.
The waves giggle, a bubbly tease,
As I trip over sand, oh what a breeze!

Evening's Caress

The sun, it slips like ice cream on a cone,
Painting the sky, like a magician's throne.
Crabs do the hustle, wiggling around,
As I trip on my towel, spread out on the ground.

Coconut drinks with tiny umbrellas,
I raise a toast to the dancing fella.
Fireflies join in a silly parade,
Reminding me just how much I've made!

Where the Sky Meets the Sea

Waves wave back, like an old friend seen,
Salty air wraps me like a jellybean.
Seagulls squawk, they must have a plan,
While I wiggle my toes in the fine golden sand.

A sunset selfie with a playful crab,
It pinches my cheeks, oh, what a jab!
The tides roll in, they prefer the fun,
While I sing loudly, "Hey, look, I'm the one!"

A Serenade of the Twilight

Stars peek out, playing hide and seek,
While glowworms twinkle, oh so unique.
Moonbeams dance on the ocean's face,
I battle a shadow, loses the race.

These breezy nights with their charming lights,
Full of laughter, and silly delights.
A boisterous tune from the waves' own band,
While I lose my flip-flop in the sand!

Sands of Time Clothed in Night

As day gets tipsy, in hues of bright,
The beach ball rolls, a merry sight.
Crabs do the dance, in a clumsy show,
While seagulls squawk, "Hey, watch me go!"

The sun takes a bow, with a wink and grin,
A beach towel battles, no one will win.
The flip-flops flee from the sandy fight,
As laughter spins beneath the twilight.

Footprints Under the Evening Glow

Footprints scattered like a bread crumb trail,
Chasing a jellyfish, oh what a fail!
The waves giggle softly, tickling the toes,
While time swims away, in its own little prose.

The shells hold secrets of a midnight feast,
Seagulls debate who gets the most least.
Sandcastles crumble, like some silly dream,
Under the moon, where the beach pixies gleam.

The Last Light of a Distant Star

A star winks down, in a tipsy haze,
While flip-flops tap-dance in evening's blaze.
The tide whispers tales of the grand and the small,
As we giggle at shadows that stretch and sprawl.

The drinks in our cups dance with the breeze,
Sipping on laughter, feeling so at ease.
Fireflies join in for a shimmering laugh,
As we joke about life, in this nighttime bath.

Fragrance of Dusk and Warm Tides

The salty air puts a twist on our curls,
While laughter takes flight in a swirl of swirls.
A beach umbrella flips, like a hat gone wild,
And the sand sticks to all, just like a child.

The dusk brings out the shimmy in the night,
Where every shadow's a friend, quite a sight.
With warm tides teasing our toes in play,
We dance with the stars, come what may!

Whispers of Dusk's Embrace

As the day wraps up, it gives a grin,
The sun winks at clouds, it's ready to spin.
A parrot's karaoke, the crickets' delight,
All dance together, oh what a sight!

Palm trees gossip, their leaves in a sway,
While flip-flops giggle, just floating away.
A pineapple party, with drinks served in style,
Even the coconuts chuckle, for a while.

Melodies Beneath the Evening Sky

The stars take a bow, as the moon starts to rise,
Launches a concert, surprise after surprise.
The cocktails do tango, with cocktails on ice,
While shrimp on the grill declare, 'Ain't life nice!'

Frisbees soar high, like dreams in the air,
Turns out they're landing on grandma's grey hair.
A dog starts to howl, thinking he's a bard,
While everyone laughs—it's a celebration yard!

Golden Horizons and Velvet Dreams

The day melts away in a neon flair,
Sunsets turn gold, like a heartfelt dare.
Flip-flops parade while the ice cream melts,
And jellyfish join in where laughter is felt.

The hammock sways low, a snore escapes thin,
A crab passes judgment, 'You shouldn't have been!'
Seagulls join in with their best serenade,
While the sandman is loading his dreams for the trade.

Celestial Canvas of Nightfall

Canvas of colors, paint splatters bright,
A painter's pursuit in the fading daylight.
The breeze tells a joke, the ocean replies,
With waves of applause under starlit skies.

Campfire confessions, with marshmallows toasted,
The ghost of a fish, or so they all boasted.
As laughter ignites in the cool evening air,
Every little moment declares, 'Joy is rare!'

Mirage of Evening

On sandy shores, a drink in hand,
A seagull steals my snack, oh man!
With laughter echoing in the breeze,
I trip on flip-flops, fall to my knees.

The sky's ablaze, a brilliant show,
While crabs dance sideways, putting on a glow.
I wave to clouds, they giggle back,
As I sip my drink and lose my snack.

Luminous Dreams

Stars peek out like giggly sprites,
Drawing pictures of comical sights.
A dolphin's joke, a fishy pun,
While I chuckle, my fun's just begun.

The moon's a disco ball up high,
Reflecting laughter from the sky.
With every twinkle, the jokes grow bolder,
As the night unfolds its sparkling folder.

The Ocean's Canvas

Waves paint stories on the sand,
As I try to build with a clumsy hand.
My castle's leaning, oh what a sight,
The tide is laughing, 'you can't win this fight!'

The sun dips low, a ball of gold,
While octopuses giggle, jokes unfold.
With every splash, they're telling tales,
Of silly sailors and their failed sails.

When Day Meets Night

As day gives way, the sky's ablaze,
A parrot squawks in a colorful craze.
I trip on starfish strewn about,
And question loudly, what's that about?

Fireflies blink, they crowd around,
While I dance goofy on the ground.
"Join me," I shout, to a nearby sprite,
As we jig together on that fateful night.

A Gentle Caress of Dusk

As daylight slips, the crabs all dance,
In search of snacks, they take a chance.
The sun, a cheeky orange ball,
Winks at the waves—come catch my fall!

With cocktails in hand, they toast the shade,
While seagulls plot a food parade.
The breeze brings laughter, a playful tease,
As sunburned faces exchange stories with ease.

Heaven's Palette Beyond the Water

A painter's brush with shades of fun,
Slathers the sky as day is done.
Pineapple hats and flip-flop cheer,
We raise our cups, let's make it clear!

The parrots squawk in vibrant hues,
While we all argue about our shoes.
The ocean giggles with every wave,
Who knew the sunset had a rave?

Evening's Embrace in Paradise

Beneath the palms, we gather round,
With spicy snacks and laughter loud.
Fireflies join, like tiny lights,
Dancing among our wild delights.

The horizon blushes in purple flair,
As we all trip over beach chair glare.
"Who placed that there?" we shout in glee,
While the moon smirks, "It wasn't me!"

Stars Tucked in the Sea's Fabric

The twinkling gems drop from the sky,
As jellyfish float and wink goodbye.
We search for constellations bright,
While sunscreen still glistens in the night.

Comets streak as we munch on fries,
While crabs critique our laughing cries.
The glowing sea, a perfect stage,
Where wisdom's lost in endless age.

A Tapestry of Light and Shadow

Colors spill across the sky,
As I hold my drink up high.
Did the clouds just say hello?
Or was it just my inner glow?

Dancing shadows on the ground,
Tiptoe, twirl, without a sound.
A palm frond waves, oh so sly,
Who needs a DJ? Just let them fly!

The sun's wearing shades, what a sight,
While I try to catch that kite.
With laughter louder than the waves,
We're like fish in party caves!

A vibrant blend, a lively scene,
Wishing that I was a jelly bean.
As night arrives with a funky beat,
Let's groove 'til we can't feel our feet!

Bottle Palm Shadows at Dusk

The shadows stretch, they make me grin,
As bottle palms wear silly skin.
"Is that a hat?" I quip with glee,
Or just a squirrel, must be a spree!

The horizon blushes, cheeks all red,
While my friends play 'who's the fastest head?'
Caught in laughter, my drink gets wet,
Oops, who knew coconut was a threat?

A breeze whispers with a cheeky tone,
"Hey buddy, you're not alone!"
As gulls pass by, they steal my fry,
A seagull thief, oh my oh my!

The sky is a canvas, all bright and bold,
And my stories are being retold.
With every chime of a distant bell,
I think we've cast quite the spell!

The Ocean's Breathy Secrets

Waves tickle shores with playful sighs,
As I look out for a fish that flies.
The sea whispers tales of old and new,
But all I hear is 'snack time' too!

Bubbles burst in giggles bright,
As crabs parade in their silly fight.
"Who wore it better?" a clam will yell,
I just hope they won't be in my shell!

Sun-kissed moments in ocean spray,
As laughter dances and waves sway.
I think I caught a mermaid's wink,
Or was it just a fish with a blink?

The horizon's hiding snacks galore,
With every splash, I want more.
So let's toast to tides and salty fries,
And pickled dreams with starry skies!

Nightfall's Gentle Caress

As night tiptoes in with a grin,
The stars blink once, then we begin.
Moonbeams slide down, a lovely sight,
Catching toes in soft, silvery light.

Fireflies join in the sparkly game,
Deciding which one should take the fame.
"Hey there, buddy, shine it bright!
Let's see who'll dance until daylight!"

The ocean whispers lullabies sweet,
As I attempt to tap my feet.
A clam in a tux, thinks it's a show,
But don't ask me, I'm just here for the glow!

With coconuts clinking, we laugh and sway,
Sharing secrets at the end of the day.
So here's to wishes on every star,
And the joy we find, just being bizarre!

Moonlit Shores

On shores where waves do crash and play,
A crab in shorts kicks sand away.
The moon grins down with a cheeky face,
While beach balls bounce at a comical pace.

Seagulls squawk their raucous tune,
Thinking they're stars 'neath the glowing moon.
Sandcastles wobble with a silly sway,
As the tide whispers, 'Hey, not today!'

Flip-flops dance like they're on the run,
A party awaits while the day is done.
With laughter echoing through the night,
Even the stars wink in sheer delight.

So raise your drink, toast the critters,
To funny memories and sandy glitter.
Let's kick up our heels, don't be shy,
The shoreline's alive, just you and I.

Afterglow Secrets

When the sun dips low, it's quite the sight,
Chasing away the day, igniting the night.
Fruits and drinks line up on the spread,
While ants plot schemes to steal the bread.

A parrot giggles in the coconut tree,
Yelling, 'Free snacks! Come and see!'
The firewood crackles, a comical flare,
While friends trip over a beach chair's dare.

Stars peek out, ready for a laugh,
A starfish jokes, 'I'm the best half!'
Secret whispers of fruity delight,
Bubbles of giggles dance out of sight.

So let's spill secrets till morning light,
With a punchline here and a goofy bite.
In afterglow's warmth, we'll surely stay,
Creating memories in a wacky way.

Starry Infinity

Under the cosmos, so vast and bright,
Fireflies flicker, winking with delight.
A raccoon rummages for snacks in the sand,
Performing stand-up, his fans in high demand.

The stars are laughter, twinkling above,
While owls hoot out tunes filled with love.
A comet zips past, says, 'Howdy, friend!'
In the night's embrace, silliness won't end.

Cartwheeling crabs put on a show,
As the tide pulls back, the crowd goes 'Whoa!'
The moon rolls eyes, switching to a grin,
As laughter erupts from deep within.

In infinity's clasp, we find our glee,
With goofy moments where quirks run free.
So let the stars guide our playful spree,
In the dance of the night, wild and carefree.

The Dance of the Fireflies

In the garden where giggles bloom,
Fireflies gather, lighting up the gloom.
They twist and twirl like a silly ballet,
While the frogs start singing, 'Come join the fray!'

A grasshopper leaps with a comedic flair,
Making the daisies shout, 'Hey, beware!'
Each flicker and hop adds to the charm,
While night creeps in with its gentle arms.

A breeze whispers secrets, oh-so-fine,
As owls chuckle, enjoying the wine.
The moon drops in, wearing shades of gold,
To witness the antics, both brave and bold.

So dance with the fireflies, join the fun,
Let laughter echo 'til the rise of the sun.
In this whimsical world, we'll find our way,
With joy in each step, come what may.

Tranquil Reflections

A parrot squawks a warning sign,
As I juggle coconuts on the line.
The ocean winks at my flailing limbs,
While fish swim by, sharing my whims.

The palm trees sway like they're laughing loud,
At my dance moves, not fit for a crowd.
With a flip and a flop, I trip on my toes,
The sunset chuckles, 'Oh, how it goes!'

A hammock's nest is where I should stay,
But I leap like a frog in a joyous ballet.
The colors burst like a piñata's cheer,
As I giggle at nature sipping her beer.

Chasing the Horizon

I set out to catch a runaway sun,
With flip-flops flying, oh what fun!
Racing the waves, I slip and I slide,
Dancing with shadows, I can't hide.

The colors blend like a cosmic joke,
While clouds puff up like a kitchen smoke.
I reach for the sky, what a silly game,
But laughter erupts, it calls my name.

A crab joins in, with claws in the air,
As if to say, 'Hey, life's unfair!'
We prance on the shore, in a comic chase,
I laugh like a fool, with crabs in the race.

Nocturnal Blossoms

Under the stars, a serenade sings,
As a raccoon debates if it wants to bring
A snack from the fridge, oh what a scene,
As fireflies wink, like they're on a screen.

The moon is a disco ball tonight,
Shining on plants that are feeling quite bright.
I stumble upon flowers that bloom in a jest,
Where bees throw rave parties, all up in their fest.

I spot a cat that's eyeing a mouse,
But the mouse is too busy to care or to douse.
Under the stars, life giggles away,
As the night blossoms in wild, funny play.

Gentle Breezes and Burning Skies

On a beach where flip-flops reign supreme,
The wind plays tricks—a prankish theme.
My hat takes off, it flies with a whirr,
While seagulls laugh at my fashionable stir.

The sunset's hues are competing for fame,
While I try to catch the end of the game.
But every gust sends me twirling anew,
With laughter in air, as I wave to the crew.

The sand tickles toes with mischievous glee,
Is this a dance or just foolery?
With every gust, my troubles take flight,
While the sun dips low, ending a whimsical night.

Twilight's Serenade on Silken Waves

As the sun dips down with a wink,
The dolphins play, giving us a wink.
Umbrella drinks spill from the sand,
While seagulls laugh with a comical band.

Flip-flops flying in a crazy dance,
While we attempt a clumsy romance.
The tide rolls in, a mischievous mate,
As we chase the waves, our clumsiness great.

Fishermen's tales stretch under the sky,
Caught a big one? Oh, what a lie!
While crabs do the cha-cha, we cheer,
It's the best kind of chaos, I do declare!

From shore to star, the laughter flows,
With coconut hats and ridiculous toes.
As night creeps in, our fun doesn't end,
For under the moon, we make silly friends.

Stars in the Lullaby of the Ocean

Waves crash down like a bumpy drum,
As crabs moonwalk, we laugh—they're so dumb.
A blanket of sky filled with twinkling jokes,
Even the tides grin, full of bespoke folks.

Shells whisper secrets that make us giggle,
Float like jellyfish but then we wiggle.
Stars twinkle like lights on a goofy tree,
While we chase fireflies, wild and carefree.

A sandcastle crumbles, splendorous and grand,
While beach towels turn to a fortress land.
The night is young with laughter so loud,
Like birds in pajamas, we're definitely proud.

Under this whimsy, let worries take flight,
In the dance of the waves, everything's right.
With a sprinkle of joy and a pinch of flair,
We sing out to the universe without a care!

Radiance at the Edge of Tomorrow

Day's final act, a clumsy bow,
While palm trees laugh, 'What a show, wow!'
We sit on the sand, popcorn in hand,
As fireflies jiggle across the expanse planned.

The horizon blushes, a cheeky tease,
While sandcastles groan, begging for ease.
We chase a lost flip-flop, what a sight,
Making memories in the fading light.

Bikinis and board shorts start to gleam,
As we dance in our sunscreen, no refined theme.
The breeze tells tales, we can't help but sway,
With each silly move, we brighten the day.

Tomorrow's laughter lies just beyond,
In this whimsical place where we all respond.
With sunburns and giggles, we take our leave,
In the radiance of fun, we truly believe.

Nocturnal Blooms and Ocean Hues

The moon grins bright with a puffy face,
While crabs have a meeting, plotting their race.
We joke with the stars, their lights on the roam,
Like kids in a candy shop, this beach is our home.

Petunias sway in a breezy chat,
Giggling with daisies, 'Look at that cat!'
He prances around like he owns the shore,
Leaving paw prints in laughter, who could ask for more?

The ocean hums a ridiculous tune,
As jellyfish jiggle, it's quite a cartoon.
We gather up shells, they sing as we walk,
A nostalgic chorus filled with sea talk.

In this calm chaos, with bright hues so bold,
We find joy in wonders, both new and old.
With laughter like bubbles, we make the night sing,
In the blooms of the night, oh, what joy they bring!

Sunkissed Moments Gone by Night

The sun yells, 'I want a break!'
The horizon is on a sunlit hike.
Palms wave like they're on a stage,
While flip-flops dance, full of rage.

The sky spills juice in colors bold,
Fish gossip, their tales retold.
A crab wears shades, looks pretty fly,
While seagulls squawk, 'Let's say goodbye!'

Clouds tickle the sun with a grin,
As night falls, let the laughter begin.
Stars wink, 'Hey! Who turned off the light?'
The moon snickers, 'Just hold on tight!'

So raise a glass, let's make a toast,
To fading light and that funny coast.
With smiles stretched wide and hearts in flight,
We'll laugh until the morning light!

Driftwood Dreams in Starlight

On a beach with driftwood and shells,
Seagulls tell tales that sound like spells.
A fish on a skateboard zooms by,
Shouting, 'Catch me if you can, oh my!'

The tide pulls in, the waves go 'Moo!'
Who knew the ocean could act like you?
Starfish dance, they know the cheat,
As crabs hold hands and tap their feet.

With sand in our toes, we laugh and play,
Count the stars, they're here to stay.
A coconut drinks, straws all around,
While jellyfish bounce to the sound.

So let's build a castle and make it grand,
With turrets of laughter, bright as the sand.
When dreams collide in the moonlit air,
We'll drift in our thoughts, without a care!

A Canvas of Celestial Whispers

The sky paints secrets in shades so bright,
As dolphins perform their evening flight.
While stars chase the sun behind a tree,
A chirping cricket sings, 'You're free!'

Clouds wear pajamas, all snug and neat,
While fireflies dance, with tiny feet.
The sunfish giggles, a bubble joke,
While everyone beams, 'What a poke!'

The moon wears glasses, so wise and round,
While lazy lightning bugs float around.
The universe winks, a playful tease,
As laughter floats on every breeze.

In this gallery of dreams and glee,
Let's paint our nights with wild esprit.
When constellations smile and play,
We'll dance through the night till break of day!

Flickers of Cornflower Blue

In the dusk, colors swirl, take flight,
Cornflower blue, oh what a sight!
A parrot laughs, squawking in delight,
As we all groove in the fading light.

A coconut falls with a thump and roll,
While a raccoon tries to steal the whole bowl.
The crabs throw a party, how absurd,
With shrimp as DJs, haven't you heard?

The stars giggle, trying on their clothes,
While sleepy owls strike odd, funny poses.
In waves that whisper secrets of old,
We flip like pancakes, brave and bold.

So here's to laughter in the evening's hue,
In moments like this, you find the clues.
We'll celebrate life amidst the fun,
Until the last flicker bids us adieu!

Echoes of Light Where Waves Meet

The sun slips down, a giant coin,
Seagulls laugh, they think it's a join.
Flip-flops flying, a dance in mirth,
Sand between toes, the jesters of earth.

A crab in shades, strutting his stuff,
While beach balls bounce, they play it rough.
Waves whisper tales, of jellyfish crew,
Who ask for a snack, would you like one too?

Palm trees nodding, quite the chatter,
As kids try to build, but seagulls scatter.
The horizon's a canvas, splashed with cheer,
Where laughter echoes, loud and clear.

There's a dog that barks with flair and function,
Chasing his tail, a silly production.
As the colors blend, a punchline unfolds,
Nature's comedy show, never gets old.

Dusk's Kiss on Sandy Shores

The sky's a painter, throws on a show,
While kids in the sand, play most don't know.
Sandcastles tumble, with each wave's tease,
As if Mother Nature's got a sense of ease.

A ladybug sails on a crab that's a boat,
While someone yells, 'Do you think it will float?'
The tide comes in, the moon winks bright,
As if to say, 'Hold on, it's a fright!'

A starfish that's sunbathing boasts of his tan,
While a beach umbrella plans its escape, man!
The waves clap hands, a rhythm they find,
While giggles erupt, the best kind of bind.

With the curtain of night, the banter rolls free,
As lanterns take flight, like jellyfish glee.
Every joke told, from the heart full of fun,
In this joyful dance, there's never just one!

Cosmic Dreams Beneath the Palms

Underneath shade where the shadows jump,
Roaches in hula skirts—such a lump!
The moon hangs low, like a giant pie,
While crickets croon their symphonic sigh.

A raccoon with flair steals a chip or two,
Laughing aloud, as if saying 'Who knew?'
Starry-eyed dreams float in drink cups spilled,
As constellations burp, the night is grilled.

The breeze tells secrets, of giggles and cheese,
While owls hoot punches, with perfect ease.
A party of fireflies buzz with delight,
In sync with the dance, 'til their batteries light.

The palms sway gently, a disco in bloom,
Disguised are the stars, in the night's costume.
In this realm of fun, let imagination reign,
With laughter and cheer, we've all gone insane!

Gold Fades to Night's Embrace

Last rays of gold, a spotlight's allure,
Boys flying kites, while girls laugh for sure.
A jelly on the shore, with jellybean dreams,
Frolicking in fun, bursting at the seams.

The crab on the run, in a game of tag,
While seagulls plot schemes, with a winged brag.
The horizon blushes, with blushes so bright,
As laughter rings clear, in the coming night.

Driftwood delight, a wizard's leftover,
Imagination flies, like a high-flying rover.
With sand in their hair, and smiles that gleam,
As the waves start to dance, it's a dream of a dream.

A thunderstorm chuckles, 'Oh, what a place!'
As we toast to the twilight, with cupcakes of grace.
In the playful world where shadows tease,
The fun never ends; it's a joyous breeze.

Moonlight's Mirror on Silver Sands

The moon's a disco ball, don't you see?
Wave a fin, dance like a dolphin, whee!
Seashells join the conga line at night,
While crabs do the twist, oh what a sight!

A sandcastle prince shimmies with flair,
His crown made of shells, he doesn't care.
Starfish applaud from their sandy throne,
While jellyfish groove, all on their own!

The night turns to giggles, under the glow,
As flip-flops become shuttles, to and fro.
Gulls sing silly songs, in comical tones,
While we share fresh coconuts with ice cream cones!

So let's toast to the tides as they swirl around,
With laughter that echoes, a joyful sound.
For in this bright rhythm, we'll take a chance,
To dance with the waves in a merry glance!

Horizons Burning Bright

The sun's a giant pancake on the grill,
While seagulls fly past, giving us a thrill.
The sky's a mixed-up palette of delight,
A watercolor rainbow, oh what a sight!

Surfboards are laughing, wobbling in waves,
As the tide tells secrets, the beach still craves.
Sandcastles whisper, 'Watch us compete!'
While beach balls giggle, rolling in the heat.

Ice cream melts faster than tales we can spin,
While crabs play peek-a-boo, hiding their grin.
Barbecue smoke swirls up to the sky,
As hot dogs do somersaults, oh my, oh my!

When day turns to night and shadows take stand,
The horizons conspire, concocting the band.
So join in the madness, let laughter ignite,
As we revel in moments that feel so right!

The Star-Crafted Sea

Stars like popcorn scatter on dark waves,
While fish wear tuxedos, feeling quite brave.
The ocean's a stage where silliness thrives,
As dolphins all cheer, with joy in their dives!

Octopuses juggle, with each floppy limb,
While sea turtles moonwalk, on a whim.
The waves sing sweet serenades to the shore,
As crabs tap their claws, always wanting more!

Bubbles float up, like giggles in air,
While pirate parrots squawk, without a care.
The night is a circus, with stars in a row,
As we laugh with the sea, letting our hearts glow!

So lift up your voice, let joy be the key,
Dance with the currents, feel wild and free.
For in this bright wonder, where smiles are rife,
Every wave tells a joke—what a fun life!

Where Dusk Meets Endless Waves

As dusk tiptoes in with a wink and a grin,
The waves play tag, with laughter, they spin.
A flamingo on stilts strolls down the shore,
While snails on their scooters call out for more!

The sun puts on sunglasses, ready to chill,
While beach umbrellas sway, it's quite the thrill.
Seashells gossip about the day's silly blunders,
As moonlight unfolds with its soft, shimmering wonders.

Tide pools are treasures, where giggles abound,
With starfish performing - what a joy found!
As the horizon waves goodnight to the sun,
The laughter of dusk has only begun!

So gather your friends, let's share all our dreams,
In this magical moment, where nothing's as it seems.
With snacks from the cooler and joy in our hearts,
We'll dance with the ocean, where laughter imparts!

Saffron Horizons

The sky drips gold like the dinner plate,
Caught in a heat wave, we dance with fate.
We throw our drinks in a lemony cheer,
While seagulls squawk like they own the pier.

Sunburned noses wave in the breeze,
As flip-flops flop while the sunset teases.
A laugh breaks free, like a runaway kite,
Landing in waves, oh what a sight!

Indigo Whispers

In twilight's cloak, a cool breeze sighs,
Belly laughs echo under purple skies.
We sip on coconuts with paper straws,
While the crabs scamper, defying all laws.

The stars peek out, a curious crew,
Like shy comedians waiting to debut.
With laughter galore, it's quite the show,
As we play bingo with fireflies in tow.

Shimmering Light on the Shoreline

Footprints squish in the sand so fine,
As we build castles with iced lemonade—divine!
Waves crash and giggle, they splash and they race,
Suddenly, it's a wet t-shirt contest face!

With jellyfish winking as they drift by,
We pretend to paddle, yet barely fly.
Sunbaked snacks and mango delight,
Sandy and sticky, oh, what a night!

Moments Before the Stars Awaken

Just before dusk, the mischief begins,
With monkeys plotting hijinks, wearing grins.
We search for shells, ooh, look at this one!
A perfect disguise for a runaway stun!

As colors collide and clouds do the twist,
We chant silly songs, you won't want to miss.
The sky's got jokes, as shadows take flight,
In this moment, we laugh into the night!

Embered Skies and Moonlit Bliss

Under the embers, we roast marshmallow dreams,
With sticky fingers and chocolate seams.
Our jokes get sillier with every s'more,
As laughter erupts, oh, who could ask for more?

Glow sticks wiggle and dance in delight,
The ocean hums tunes through the velvety night.
While fireflies join with a flickering dance,
We toast to the moment, oh, what a chance!

Echoes of the Sun

The day waves goodbye, with a cheeky grin,
As shadows dance, let the laughter begin.
The sky splashes colors like ice cream on toast,
While crabs do the cha-cha, we cheer and we boast.

Palm trees sway as if they've had too much rum,
And seagulls squawk tunes, oh they think they're so dumb.
Flip-flops are squeaking, they've lost all their flair,
As we search for warmth in the breeze that is rare.

With drinks in our hands, we decide we're all chefs,
Trying to grill snacks with our clumsy old steps.
The fire's too high, and the smoke's in our eyes,
We cough and we giggle, our laughter will rise.

As lights start to twinkle and shades take their cue,
We trade all our worries for joy like a stew.
So grab a good friend, let's dance with the night,
For life is a party, and it's feeling so right!

A Palette for the Night

The sun dips low in a ridiculous hat,
Mixing up oranges and splashes of fat.
The waves are like cushions, they're soft and they play,
While crickets recite poems in a silly way.

Stars giggle down, they've had way too much fun,
Playing hide and seek with the light from the sun.
A coconut shimmies, it wants in the dance,
As the moon pulls strings, like it's stuck in a trance.

The breeze carries whispers of secrets to share,
With fish on the shore grinning with a hot flair.
A glow-in-the-dark crab waves, "Hey, guess my name!"
While dolphins jump in, joining in on the game.

The night hums a tune from a faraway place,
While we twirl on the sand, with smiles on our face.
A canvas of giggles, of wishes and dreams,
As wild as the ocean, and bursting with beams!

Gleaming Sands

Sandy toes wiggle as the sun starts to fade,
Making room for a party, no need for a trade.
With shovels and pails, we all start to cheer,
Building sandcastles, oh dear, what a sphere!

The waves laugh along with their foamy embrace,
As we jest with the shells, wondering their case.
Are they royalty or just beach bums at play?
Plotting big schemes as they lounge every day?

Our towels join forces, a colorful crew,
Declaring a fashion show—oh, who wears what hue?
With crab judges critiquing our sunburnt parade,
We laugh till we snort, such a fine charade.

When night falls, the stars tell absurd little tales,
Of pirates who danced with imaginary whales.
So grab a big s'more and toast it just right,
In this gleaming sand world, our joy takes to flight!

Solstice Reverie

The sun pulls a prank, shining bright with a flare,
While fish swim in circles, as if they don't care.
A hammock's a throne, for the nap of the year,
As stories of llamas tap dance in our ear.

The evening parade starts with squirrels in capes,
Accompanied by sea turtles, oh what silly shapes!
With laughter contagious, we're covered in bliss,
As we try to catch fireflies, oh what a miss!

The moon looks amused, peeking over the trees,
While crabs serenade us, with songs in the breeze.
"Chase me!" they shout, as they scuttle away,
Transforming our night into whimsical play.

So let's raise our glasses to moments so bright,
To memories painted in laughter and light.
As the stars shimmer gently, we gather our cheer,
In this merry old madness, all worries disappear!

The Last Kiss of Daylight

The sun pulls a prank, it's time for a break,
Slipping behind clouds, with a mischievous shake.
The seagulls all giggle, as they dive for a snack,
While tourists all fumble with their towels out back.

Flip-flops go flying, oh what a sight,
As laughter erupts in the fading light.
A coconut falls, a gentle thud,
Was that a bird? Or just a dud?

Life's a beach party where jokes never end,
As flip-flops and laughter blend and bend.
Umbrellas start closing, drinks spill in the sand,
And sunset's last blush takes a slap on the hand.

When the twilight arrives, with its glittery cheer,
We dance like the stars—slightly tipsy, my dear.
With jellyfish waltzing and dolphins that swoon,
We wave goodbye to the day—and hello to the moon!

Under the Coral-Colored Skies

Under skies painted pink and a hint of bright lime,
We gather for selfies, all caught up in rhyme.
A pineapple's wearing the strangest of hats,
While beach towels gossip and sunburns chat stats.

The crabs form a conga, what a sight to behold,
As we toss back our drinks, getting brave and bold.
Golden sands tickle our toes, what a thrill,
While whispers of evening bring a silly chill.

The laughter keeps rising as waves sway in grace,
With a splash from a buddy who just slipped in place.
Fireflies join in, with their sparkles and zings,
And the palm trees are swaying like they've got strings.

Under coral hues, we're all mischief and fun,
With flip-flops a-clapping 'til the day is done.
A giggle, a wiggle, let's dance without cares,
In this wild carnival where sand's stuck in our hair!

Celestial Lanterns Dance

Look at those twinkling lights starting to sway,
Is that a party up there, or a cosmic ballet?
The stars are all dressed in their shiniest gowns,
While aliens giggle and juggle their crowns.

A moonbeam slips by, with a wink and a smile,
As jellybean rockets speed past with style.
A fish in a top hat takes the stage in delight,
To serenade fireflies on this starry night.

The night grows thicker with sparkling drama,
As the Milky Way shines like a cosmic panorama.
With popcorn for thoughts in a nebula hull,
We float on the clouds, feeling light as a lull.

"Play your tunes!" we cheer, as the heavens combust,
While meteors race, dripping stardust!
Together we sway as the planets take flight,
Chasing giggles galore through this whimsical night!

Twilight Reflections in Grains of Sand

As the sun winks goodbye, colors shimmer and blend,
The grains of the shore seem to dance with a friend.
Each step brings a giggle, as we squish in the mold,
Building castles complete with a unicorn's gold.

The tides roll in, bringing tales from afar,
Shells echo laughter under the sea's bizarre.
A seagull steals fries from a poor little child,
And we can't help but laugh as the kid screams in wild.

The breeze tells of stories while we sip from a cup,
With tiny umbrellas where the fun never stops.
As the light fades out, the shadows creep in,
But here comes a crab—let the games now begin!

With reflections of joy sparkling bright in the sand,
We dance through the twilight, a comical band.
Another day edges to slumber's sweet call,
But fun rolls on in the twilight for all!

The Dance of Twilight and Stillness

As the day waves goodbye with a cheerful grin,
Crabs start to shimmy, let the fun begin.
Colors explode, like a tropical piñata,
While seagulls debate if they'll join the cha-cha.

Palm trees sway, calling their friends,
The sun plops down, but the party never ends.
Laughter erupts like a fizzy drink,
As fish make splashes, and dolphins wink.

Dreams Cradled by a Diamond Sky

The stars twinkle over like jolly little sprites,
They gossip and giggle, sharing old flights.
A crab in a tux wants to star in a play,
While the moon laughs so hard it lights up the bay.

The night is a canvas, splashed with delight,
Where dreams play hide-and-seek in the night.
A breeze sings softly, tickling the grass,
While flamingos dance, with flair, they all pass.

Golden Horizons

The horizon blushes, bright as a flame,
With flair like a dancer, it's never the same.
Beach balls go bouncing past every face,
While sunsets practice their intricate grace.

Surfboards are plotting their next funny trick,
As the sun yawns wide, it's no longer slick.
A picnic unfolds with a splash of delight,
And the parrots squawk, 'It's a marvelous night!'

Whispering Waves

Waves giggle softly as they tickle the beach,
Whispering secrets only they can teach.
The seaweed dances, all tangled and spry,
While surfers share tales of how high they can fly.

The horizon dips low, a playful wink,
Seashells giggle, 'Come on, don't blink!'
As the coconut drinks want a round of their own,
In the laughter of waves, we all feel at home.

www.ingramcontent.com/pod-product-compliance
Lightning Source LLC
Chambersburg PA
CBHW072134070526
44585CB00016B/1674